From Artistic To Entrepreneur

Turn Your Creativity

Into a Thriving Online Business

Using the Etsy Platform

Mandy Lee

ISBN: 0-9990263-1-3
ISBN-13: 978-0-9990263-1-1

DEDICATION

To Jeremy.
My husband, my heart, my rock,
my constant support,
and my best friend… with so many benefits.
I couldn't have done it without you.

And to my entire family,
who have always and unconditionally
supported my creative endeavors.
I consider myself truly lucky
to have been born into this tribe.

ACKNOWLEDGMENTS

Thank you to my beta readers,
my "Magnificent Seven"!

Kelly Carlin
Gina Gargone
Skye Gibbins
Christy Howell
Jeremy Jones
Erin Sanborn
Tanra West

Input from each one of you was invaluable
to the making of this book.
I am truly grateful for your time,
your discerning intellect,
and your honest insight.

CONTENTS

Introduction 1

The Birth Of A Business 8

Etsy Defined 18

The Entrepreneurial Secret To Success 24

Overwhelm 34

Go Inside 41

What To Sell 48

How To Sell Your Stuff 54

Your Space 63

Taking Care Of Business 66

Pricing Your Work 72

Making Money 78

Photography 85

Setting Up Your Shop 104

Shipping 114

Customer Service 126

Be Patient And Grow 132

Resources 136

About The Author 139

Why then the world's mine oyster,
which I with sword will open.

WILLIAM SHAKESPEARE

INTRODUCTION

There has never been a better time in the history of the world to be an entrepreneur. It's an exciting time to be alive. We are in the midst of a quickly moving human evolution. Because of technology, our minds and bodies are literally adapting to new ways of functioning. We have global access to people, products, and education at our very fingertips. And everything you need to know is right there on your computer or smartphone just waiting for you to ask for it, and most of it is free.

But the rules of business and job security are changing. No longer can you rely on a college education to get you the good job that will employ you for 30 years until you retire with a gold watch and a good pension. That doesn't exist anymore. As individuals, and especially creatives, we have to look at new and innovative ways to invent our own job and income security.

This Is The Era Of The Entrepreneur.

Welcome to the guide designed to train your brain to think like an entrepreneur and follow through. This book will give you all you need to know to start your online business using Etsy, and just as critical, it will give you the mental tools to grow and maintain it. This book will make it easy for you to start out on Etsy, and starting is the most important part!

You'll even be able to open your shop for FREE!
Go to: www.FromArtisticToEntrepreneur.com for your first free 40 listings.

Now is the time to start making your own money and creating your own employment security that puts you on the path to a more independent, successful, and happy lifestyle.

While this book is geared towards the fine artist, this book is for everyone who has ever felt their soul's artistic presence and wants to explore it – from corporate CEOs to firefighters and beyond. If you've ever wanted to "make something from your creative place" and put it out there, this guide will show you how to do it with ease, comfort, and privacy.

Creativity Is The New Currency.

Technology has changed how the world does business and it is essential that you know the ways in which this can benefit you. Technology is a tool, and when used correctly, it can empower you to finally achieve the life you really want. In this new world of constant innovation, the new business model is all about the individual.

We can no longer rely on a job or even a career with someone else to secure our source of income and employment. We need to be resourceful and innovative to assure our success for ourselves and our family. Once we learn how to harness this power of global interaction and commerce, the world really can be our oyster.

To Do What You Love And Make A Great Living At It Is The Ultimate Definition Of A Successful Lifestyle.

I have always been an artist and yet, for most of my life, I never thought I could make a living at it. Somewhere early along my creative journey, I picked up the adage "poor, starving artist." And unintentionally, that became my inner dialogue, cultivating a false and disempowering belief system. It took a long time and a lot of mental work for me to change that credence. I now have a career based on my creativity and I couldn't be happier or more grateful.

This book will show you step-by-step how to easily enter the online marketplace and explore the ways that you can start a business from your artistic endeavors. I chose to illustrate this process with Etsy because it is a simple, effective, and inexpensive way to get your goods into the hands of the people who want to buy them.

The tips and tools contained here can also help you on many other business platforms – whether it be utilizing a gallery, a storefront, or traveling to craft shows to sell your wares. It's not only about how to set up your art business, but how to maintain it, both physically and more importantly, mentally.

The Infinite Power Of The Internet

I chose to write a book about this process because for years, many people, especially artists, have asked me a lot of questions about my Etsy business and my ability to employ myself. I had never written a book before, but I knew it was in me. After much online research, I found a thorough and effective

Self Publishing Course (http://bit.ly/2pdNP85), which obviously, taught me how to do it!

This book is just another example of how the internet, if utilized wisely, is the most powerful tool we have to link us to the rest of the world, get educated, do some good, and even earn a living from it all at the same time.

Afraid To Go Public

Are you nervous about exploring and then exposing your creative ideas to the world? Some of you may want to try your hand at a creative career without the judgment of your professional peers or family. With Etsy, you can create a shop and a public profile using a pen name and therefore keep your real identity private. This gives you the ultimate freedom to examine and play with your creative alter ego and make some money while you're doing it.

It's Not About Your Resources, It's About Your Resourcefulness.

If running a business were easy, everyone would do it! Yes, it will take some hard work and initiative (like most good things in life), but with the right tools and mental attitude, you can absolutely do it!

So here's your chance to get started and

finally say "Hello!" to that little voice that's been telling you all along that you should "Do your own thing and make your own money!"

As I said, there has never been a better time to be an entrepreneur. You now have a worldwide audience just waiting for you!

All you have to do is start.

Start by reading this book.

Start by looking inside yourself and honoring your creative spirit.

Start by knowing that you can do this and it's about time!

Just start!

Two roads diverged in a wood, and I -
I took the one less travelled by,
And that has made all the difference.

ROBERT FROST

THE BIRTH OF A BUSINESS

It's fascinating how an idea can come into being, how it can evolve and have a life of its own and turn into something you could never have imagined at the start.

In 2010, Jeremy Jones and I were married on the sands of the Delaware seashore. We live in Taos, New Mexico, so when we returned home we had another celebration for our local community of friends. For this postnuptial party, we built a grand stage for Jeremy's band and for the other participating musicians.

The following year, while sitting on that stage, an idea came to me. "Let's put on a Shakespeare play," I declared. Now, I was familiar with the bard's work, as I had grown up in the small Delaware town called Arden, aptly named after Shakespeare's famous forest. I grew up watching the Arden players perform outdoor Shakespeare every summer, but it had never before occurred to me to do that in my southwestern mountain home.

It seems that the moment I uttered those words out loud, people started showing up "out of the woodwork" as they say. Costumers, actors, writers and generally enthusiastic neighbors all wanted to be part of the project. And almost magically, the unexpected theater company, Teatro Serpiente, was born and it was a success. There were months of practice and preparations and then for a few weekends each summer, hundreds of locals and tourists alike descended on our lawn, sitting on folding chairs and straw bales to enjoy the theatrics. The performances were such a success in fact, that this new theater troupe, after only two years, had to move their productions elsewhere so we could have our home back!

Teatro Serpiente performs *As You Like It*
in Taos, New Mexico, 2012.

During this time, part of my clay studio became a rehearsal space, a costume shop, and a dressing room. But there was still some room for me to play with clay and make cups on my potter's wheel. When the Shakespeare plays were performed, we set up a bar in the courtyard, and for a donation you could get a beverage in one of my handmade mugs and keep the mug. Via this method and ticket sales, we raised a lot of money for a local kids' art program called NAP, the Neighborhood Art Project. It felt great to bring people together and give back to our community.

Kate Jensen and Mandy at the Serpiente Tavern.

That first year of selling mugs, I was stamping the logo of Teatro Serpiente into the wet clay. By the second year, I had learned about using fired-on decals to put text on the already glazed pieces. I put the Serpiente logo on one side and a quote from Shakespeare on the other. The mugs were a hit! Theatergoers and actors alike all wanted one. And thus, a business was born!

The first cups made for Teatro Serpiente – 2011 and 2012.

Etsy Made It Easy

I had opened an Etsy shop called Taos Gargirl back in 2009. It was a mishmash of my pottery and sculpture and my Go-Gamin'! travel game. Every once in awhile I would get a sale, but it was random and I really didn't keep up with working my shop.

After the local success of the Teatro Serpiente cups, I knew that Etsy would be a great place to sell them. So I began in earnest to make a real business out of Taos Gargirl on Etsy. I made more cups and I took photographs and I listed them. Still, initially there was not a lot of movement. But after a few months, sales picked up slowly and I was grateful. Within a few years, the cups had become my shop's most popular items so I changed my shop name to The Quoted Cup (www.etsy.com/shop/TheQuotedCup).

Fine Art Versus Commercial Art

Now, during this time I had full-time employment elsewhere, from office work to bartending. I have always done whatever it takes to make a living outside of my art. My fine art is quite unusual and unique, and so suits a more niche audience. You can see what I mean at MandyStapleford.com.

I had always felt that it was just too much pressure to rely on my fine art for income. In fact, relying on my fine art in that way changed my art – in a way I did not like. I often felt like I was making my very personal art for someone else and that was always in the back of my mind. That feeling took away from my true artistic impulses. It's why I never liked doing commissions and I will not do them now. For me, that way of making fine art is a real creativity thief.

My Taos Gargirl Etsy shop was different. This was where I could enjoy making art for someone else. It was a way for me to create and still be in my studio doing a version of what I loved. My online shop was starting to make a little money, primarily from the cups, and that felt great.

Now, I need to clarify something here; I love making my cups but I don't consider the cups, even though they are hand finished, to be my "fine art". They are my craft or my "commercial art", which is a very different animal. I make that work in a very different way and it satisfies a very different part of my creativity. Producing the cups indulges my entrepreneurial side and the enjoyment I get out of making utilitarian objects, or "art you can use," as well as utilizing creativity to make people happy.

As I grew my business, I also grew as a craftsman, an artist, and an entrepreneur. Using the Etsy platform has taught me so much about running a business. It's been an education for sure. That education has made me a better fine artist and businesswoman in that part of my life as well.

www.etsy.com/shop/TheQuotedCup

The Quoted Cup

I enjoy making utilitarian items because I believe that we should surround ourselves with beauty no matter what we are doing. From the kitchen to the bathroom, the more handmade stuff, the better. Plus, I believe that it's just good karma to support artists whenever you can! Etsy is a good platform to learn not only about business, but also about how to connect with the outside world and interact with it by way of your creative talents!

My customers love The Quoted Cup for a number of reasons. First off, the quality of my wares is exceptional. I produce unique and well-made functional art that is customizable as well as very affordable. The cups and mugs are cast from a high temperature white clay, so they are sleek and beautiful as well as durable. Because I hand glaze each cup with my specially formulated shino glazes, the firing makes every piece one-of-a-kind, yet the similar cast forms make for beautiful sets. The multitude of quotes that I offer appeal to a wide range of ages and personalities, and I'm continually adding to my quote collection. I also offer the ability to individually tailor specific quotes on each cup. This allows my customers to create with me and make something truly personal to them, whether it be for themselves or for a gift.

The Quoted Cup also succeeds due to my commitment to provide exceptional customer service. I go out of my way to make people happy when they buy my work. I've built a following and a reputation as a company that is reliable and pleasurable to do business with.

The Etsy Advantage

I love Etsy because it has a very simple platform that is user friendly and easy to navigate. There is also a huge community of Etsy sellers that are there for you. The platform is run well and I've always had terrific support from the company when I needed it. It is also a global platform – you literally have access to most of the world. As of the writing of this book, I sell my work in eight countries! This is exciting and would not have been possible without an online platform. But perhaps most importantly, Etsy is a very inexpensive way to start and learn how to run a business.

You don't have to quit your day job to run your shop. In fact, do not quit your day job to run your shop until your shop outdoes your day job's income consistently and you know you can rely on it! But you must make time for your shop, just like you make time, via choice or necessity, for other things you do in your life. Like any relationship, it needs to be tended to, like a garden, or it will not grow. This is something I know to be true even today as I write this, eight years after I first opened my Etsy shop.

When I "work it," it works for me.

*Our mission
is to reimagine commerce
in ways that build
a more fulfilling and
lasting world.*

THE ETSY MISSION STATEMENT

ETSY DEFINED

Etsy.com is an online marketplace, similar to eBay, but with a focus on handmade or vintage items. The first site was created in June 2005 by Rob Kalin and a few of his friends out of an apartment in Brooklyn, NY. It was launched that year and by mid 2007, it had surpassed $1.7 million dollars in sales. It is referred to as a P2P, or peer-to-peer e-commerce website. As of April 2016, the company had over 55 million registered members and connected 1.6 million active sellers to over 21 million active buyers.

Most of the goods fall into the categories of crafts, craft supplies, housewares, and even some foodstuffs like candy and baked goods.

But Etsy is more than just an online store, it's a huge, global community comprised of like-minded entrepreneurs like you. There are numerous forums and groups within the site that you can use to connect with other sellers and learn how to be a better seller yourself.

Anyone with a desire to sell their handcrafted or vintage goods can be on Etsy. The Etsy platform makes it possible for you to show your wares to a once never before accessible global audience of millions! It's pretty astounding.

Reasons to Start With Etsy

There are many ways to have an online business today, with new technologies and selling platforms being created daily. I've found that Etsy has specific advantages for the average creative person who wants to try their hand at selling on the Internet. There is so little risk involved in setting up a shop. It is a great way to enter the world of online commerce because it's so easy to start and so easy to manage.

Affordability

You have enough money to set up your first Etsy shop! Creating and opening your shop is free and then you pay just $0.20 for

each listing and that listing lasts for four months. And as I mentioned earlier, you can even begin with your first 40 listings for absolutely free at:
www.FromArtisticToEntrepreneur.com.

The fees are minimal. When you make a sale, you pay approximately 3.5% of the sale price to Etsy and another 3.5% to the financial institution that made the sale possible – e.g., PayPal, Visa, MasterCard, etc. As a fine artist who has sold work through galleries and shops, I can say with confidence that this is a very good deal. If you are selling your work in a brick and mortar space, these venues typically charge a 40%-50% commission on every sale.

The Money is the Thing

With Etsy you don't need to be responsible for someone else's credit card or possible inability to pay. Etsy handles all the financial details and makes it easy for buyers to shop with confidence by providing a safe way to pay for their purchases. They offer ten different payment options for your buyers, and Etsy even lets them pay in their local currency. All that money ends up in your local bank account on a deposit schedule that you set up.

Easy Peasy

Etsy is also easy. They have created a platform that is simple to navigate and easy to learn. Most of what you'll need to do to set up your shop is self-explanatory as you go. There are also many forums within the site where you can ask for guidance from other sellers as well as request help from the Etsy staff. All you need to do is commit to the process of your own education and success.

It's Ready When You Are

It's your time and your timeline. Unlike a brick and mortar shop, your Etsy store can be set up on your own timeline and at any hour of the day or night. You don't need to quit your day job to set up and run your store. You can make the time when it's convenient for you.

But it is important, no, *imperative*, that you *do* make time. Your success on starting and running a business on Etsy, or anywhere else, depends entirely on your commitment to the process. No matter when you decide to devote time to it, make sure that you commit to that time.

Plan It

Take out a calendar and figure out when is

your "Etsy" time… just like a job… because ultimately, that's what you want it to be, right? Don't have the time? Are you sure? Just 1-2 hours for 3-5 days a week consistently, can bring you to your selling goals quicker than you might imagine. Maybe you get up earlier in the morning or spend time after dinner, instead of watching TV. What you spend your time on is what determines your life. It's up to you, and only you. So make the time and write it down so you'll honor yourself and your dreams and commit to the practice.

No Pain Yet Plenty of Gain

You have nothing to lose. Literally. Even if you started an Etsy shop and it didn't go the way you thought it would, it would still be worth it. Think of it this way: if you committed and you followed through on your desire to create a shop and sell online, you've taken action and learned something. Hopefully, you've learned a lot! Maybe the process led you down some unexpected entrepreneurial roads. Or maybe you realized that you don't actually want to run your own business. That is a valuable lesson as well. It is never a mistake if you've allowed yourself to learn lessons. As my father once counseled me during my college years, "Half of figuring out what you want to do in life is figuring out what you don't want to do." He was so right.

Hold yourself responsible
for a higher standard
than anybody else expects of you.

HENRY WARD BEECHER

THE ENTREPRENEURIAL SECRET TO SUCCESS

Self-discipline is the biggest tool in your toolbox, at least when it comes to entrepreneurship. This is probably one of the hardest skills to master initially, as you venture into the land of being your own boss and making your own money. Once you've got self-discipline down to being a habit, running and being successful in your own business becomes so much easier. Because no matter how good your product is, no matter how hard you work or how talented you are, if you don't *go* to work, consistently, your business will fail.

So it's simple, but not necessarily easy. We have to *learn* to make ourselves work for ourselves. And like anything you haven't done before or had much experience with, it takes practice. So don't worry about getting your new habits in line right away. New habits take time to become actual habits that then become automatic behavior that you don't even have to think about.

You Have Whys

One of the most important things to ask yourself when you embark on a new challenge is: what is your compelling reason to do this in the first place? What is your purpose or your *Why*? No matter what you want to accomplish in life, the reasons *why* you want it will be a far more powerful motivator than anything else.

Do you want to learn about business, make more money, have more freedom, make a positive difference in the world, or something else? Maybe to start out, you just want to challenge yourself to create art and put it out there. Your reasons are specific to you and they are valid no matter what they are. You just need to own them, regardless of what anyone else might think.

Have A Good Why

A warning about your Why being about the money. As a business platform, yes, opening a shop is about selling your goods and making money. That said, "making money" shouldn't be your Why. Why? Because if you are only focused on making money, you will miss out on a bigger purpose for yourself. You'll miss out on focusing on what you can bring to others. You'll miss out on *enjoying* your business! I firmly believe, from personal experience, that when you do what you love and love what you do, and you do it with the best intentions for others, the money just comes. Period. Also, if you are doing it only for the money, and the money does not come in your desired time frame, you'll quit. Period.

Clarity Is King

The most important thing about your Why is clarity. You must have clarity with your dreams and desires, and then you will have a path to start on. Clarity will also keep you on the path when times get tough.

To gain clarity, start by writing the Whys down. This is essential. When you write things down it forces you to be able to describe exactly what you want. You need to really understand what it is you desire, in detail. This is important because if you don't know exactly what you want, you won't get it.

It's best to write down these goals

somewhere you can see them. A notebook is good, but having the information where you can't miss looking at it is better. Try using a whiteboard or a chalkboard. Or, find a wall and fill it with sticky notes and worksheets. Be open to your reasons changing or morphing into things you had not initially thought of. Let the process be organic and flow like a river.

Of course you want to make money, but make the focus on *why* you want the money. What will the money do for you or someone else? So, instead of saying, "I want more money," say, "I want to be able to… go on a vacation, or buy more paint brushes, or buy my kid a bicycle," etc.

Also, be specific. Say exactly how much you'd like to make, in a week, a month, a year. Otherwise, you'll find a dollar on the street and presto, you've got more money – wish fulfilled – you're done. Um, no, be specific with an amount and with a compelling Why. What will more money bring you? Write it down. This is an exciting and often challenging exercise. We think we know what we want, until we have to be specific and say it out loud.

Anchor Those Whys

I learned from Tony Robbins that once you have a detailed list of desires and the compelling Whys for each of them, you'll want to tie an emotion to each one. This is the second step in training your mind to be disciplined enough to do the work it takes to really achieve your dreams.

So, if you want more money, let's say, so that you can buy your own home, then imagine the way you will feel if you don't ever get to buy your own home, ever. Aaargh, ouch, really? Yes, really. How painful will it be if you don't get to achieve this goal? Really feel it and understand the agonizing ramifications. Write them down, this will help anchor these feelings inside you.

Now, on the flip side, what will happen if you *do* get to purchase your own home? What does that mean to you and how will that make you feel? Who else in your family will that affect? How will that empower you and affect your future? Visualize this happening for yourself and how it will feel when you are no longer renting from someone else, which, by the way, is essentially paying for *their* mortgage instead of yours. Feel it, feel that sense of accomplishment and joy. You can do this. You just have to start.

Download Worksheet #1: MY WHYS at:

www.FromArtisticToEntrepreneur.com

FROM ARTISTIC TO ENTREPRENEUR

MY WHYS

MY LIST OF REASONS TO BECOME A SUCCESSFUL ENTREPRENEUR

WORKSHEET #1

Why do I want to use my creativity to create income?

Why do I want to start an online business?

Why are my Whys good reasons?

Anchor those Whys: What will I get if I achieve my desired outcomes?

Anchor those Whys: What will happen if I choose to quit early on and don't see how far I can go?

What are my short-term goals for my online business?

What are my long-term goals for my online business?

How long am I committed to running my online business?

Own Your Time

Three simple tools to assist you with self discipline are scheduling, time management, and consistency. Use a calendar to schedule your time with running your Etsy business. Schedule how much time per day or per week you will spend doing individual tasks. If you commit and are consistent with doing these tasks, they will become habits. Once these tasks become habits, they become easier, and so does your success!

Being an entrepreneur is not for the faint of heart. It took many years for me to build The Quoted Cup into what is today, and it was absolutely worth it. Many people dream of working for themselves and being on their own schedule, but real success is the difference between dreams and actions. Those who take action to make a difference in their own lives are the ones who *do* make a difference. Sometimes, it's not the results we thought we'd get, and instead we are taken in a whole new direction that we could not have even imagined. We would never know if we had not tried.

Download Worksheet #2: MY TIME at:

www.FromArtisticToEntrepreneur.com

DAILY GOALS CALENDAR

TIME	SUN	MON	TUES	WED	THUR	FRI	SAT

NOTES: _____

_____

_____

WEEKLY GOALS CALENDAR

DAY OF THE WEEK	GOAL	TIME ALLOTTED	NOTES
SUN			
MON			
TUES			
WED			
THUR			
FRI			
SAT			

NOTES: _____

_____

_____

_____

_____

MONTHLY GOALS CALENDAR

MONTH:						
SUN	**MON**	**TUES**	**WED**	**THUR**	**FRI**	**SAT**

NOTES: _____

The thing about overwhelm is:
it's all yours.
It's yours to either succumb to or to conquer.
It's your choice.
It just takes conscious action
to achieve the latter.

MANDY LEE

OVERWHELM

In this rapidly changing world, it seems that overwhelm is the "new black." You're busy, I'm busy, everyone is busy. It's practically everyone's tagline. Holy cow, we thought computers would make our lives easier, and while they do in some ways, it goes both ways. I don't think there's a working, parenting, studying person today that doesn't feel overwhelm. Sometimes, we make ourselves so busy that we are actually subconsciously sabotaging our own success without even realizing it. The trick is to know how to recognize and handle this, and it's easier than you think.

How To Manage Overwhelm

The definition of overwhelm is to "...bury or drown beneath a huge mass." Yikes, that sounds awful. Well, you need to be able to manage that mass. You just have to get your mind around the issues in a healthy way. First of all, take the emotion out of it. Negative and fearful emotions don't serve you or anyone else and it muddies up the waters of solutions. Running a business is full of challenges, not personal attacks from the Universe. Take them for what they are and take them one at a time.

Focus your attention on your desired outcome, not the "perceived" steps to get there. I say "perceived" because when you focus only on the outcome, new ways to *achieve* your outcome will surface. This is an amazingly effective way to get where you want to go with little to no stress. This works because when you focus just on the outcome, you open yourself up to new possibilities. It's almost magical when you choose to let go and listen to that inner voice of wisdom.

Retraining your brain to always enter a situation from your *desired outcome* point of view will change the way you do almost everything. Keep practicing this and it will eventually become secondary to you. It's a surprisingly effective tool you can use to easily achieve your goals, whether it's within your relationships or your business.

Simplify

Break down your goals for the day. You'll find that if you group them into categories, they'll be less overwhelming and seem much easier to accomplish. You'll find that you don't actually have 23 things to accomplish, you have five. It's also important to attach realistic time frames to accomplish your tasks. Often, the multitude of tasks on your list break down into 10, 20 or just 30 minute assignments, not nearly as long as you initially imagined.

Example: You have orders to print, to make, to pack, and to ship. You have three new items to list and you want to share those listings on social media. You also received something back in the mail that was broken.

With a list like this, I put the similar tasks together and make a new, simpler list.

Here is an example:

1. Office
   A. Print and organize new orders – 15 minutes
   B. Create new listings
2. List social media accounts to share with later and schedule when to go online – 20 minutes
   A. Share new listings on social media – 1 hour
3. Check supplies inventory and make shopping list
   A. Raw materials – 20 minutes
   B. Shipping; boxes & tape – 10 minutes
4. Call accountant – 10 minutes
   A. Upload requested documents – 20 minutes
5. Process
   A. Make new work
   B. For new orders – 2 hours
   C. For inventory – 1 hour
6. Shipping
   A. Pack ready orders – 1 hour
   B. Create labels – 20 minutes
   C. Load car with orders for P.O. – 10 minutes
   D. Trip to ship to P.O. – 30 minutes

Total estimated time: 6 hours and 45 minutes

When you can break down your daily tasks this way, you can more easily prioritize them and get them done. This also mentally simplifies your workday.

Download Worksheet #3:
MY OUTCOMES at:
www.FromArtisticToEntrepreneur.com

MY OUTCOMES

MY DAILY END GOALS TO FOCUS ON AND ACHIEVE

From
Artistic
To
Entrepreneur

WORKSHEET #3

Today's *DAILY BEAST* to slay first: _____

The rest of my day: _____

1. OFFICE   TIME:
    A.
        1.
        2.
    B.
        1.
        2.
    C.
        1.
        2.
    D.
        1.

2. PROCESS
    A.
        1.
        2.
    B.
        1.
        2.
    C.
        1.
        2.

3. SHIPPING
    A.
        1.
        2.
    B.
        1.

TOTAL ESTIMATED TIME:

Slay The Beast First

You often have some wiggle room when you are prioritizing your tasks. When I have wiggle room, I find that the best thing to do is the "worst" thing first! Get that irksome, taxing, pain-in-the-tail chore done first. Be your own annoying and demanding boss and just *tackle it*. The *it* is whatever is on your list that you want to do least. I promise you, if you get that done and out of the way first, you'll feel a weight lifted and a new sense of freedom and energy for the rest of your day. It's like getting your Christmas shopping done by December 1st... suddenly you can sit back and enjoy the season! It's an amazing trick, really.

When you get into this kind of habit, you empower yourself to get so much more done. It's like magic. Suddenly everything else gets easier and therefore more enjoyable, and voila! You are a better entrepreneur and a happier one too. You can even schedule your leisure time. Life is good.

Now I meditate twice a day for half an hour.
In meditation, I can let go of everything.
I'm not Hugh Jackman.
I'm not a dad. I'm not a husband.
I'm just dipping into that powerful source
that creates everything.
I take a little bath in it.

HUGH JACKMAN

GO INSIDE

Another little known secret to tackle overwhelm and achieve true happiness and success in business and in life, is to not let the outside world rule your inside world. The very best way you can do that is to meditate. Yes, I said meditate! Now before you roll your eyes, please hear me out. First off, "meditate" is a loaded word for sure. It conjures up visions of overly peaceful people sitting in an impossible lotus style position with their eyes closed and their hands on their knees pointed upward, finger to thumb with an almost Mona Lisa type smile on their face, sitting for hours, maybe days, right? Yeah, that's not gonna happen. Ok, the aforementioned approach is do-able, but not necessary! Let's break this down.

I like to refer to this calming and brain-cleansing practice as a time to "Go Inside". Somewhere around mid 2015 I began dabbling in meditation. Life felt crazy and I wanted relief, and meditation seemed like a good route to try. I researched online, found different versions and different mantras to use, and I pretty much dabbled in it for about a year and a half. It was a good practice and I liked how I felt afterwards, and I did it on my own timeline.

How to Go Inside

When New Year's Eve 2016 to 2017 came along, I made a new intention. I decided to commit to the practice of Going Inside every day for a month. Now, for me, what that meant was just five or ten minutes every day. The most important part of that intention was *every day*. The amount of time was less strict, and I found that as little as five to ten minutes every single day is all the time you need to see incredible results. Of course you can increase that time to whatever you want, and I do recommend going longer if you can. But know that just five minutes daily is an easy and effective way to start and get into the habit. If you do this daily for at least 30 days, you *will* feel an inner shift towards clarity.

Just Sit

First, find a quiet space and a comfortable chair. You can sit in a bed, but sit with your back vertically straight so you do not fall asleep. You want to be comfortable, but not lazy. Next, close your eyes and focus on your breathing. I find that a great way to bring consciousness to your breathing is to start with four sets of breathing in four breaths through your nose and then out four breaths through your mouth. Start with four breathing sets like this and then breathe normally but deeply.

Find Your Mantra

Next, you want to focus on a mantra. A mantra is a phrase or word that you keep repeating silently to help you stay in the quiet place and not have your mind wander so much. Anything can be your mantra; it just needs to feel right to you. There are classic Sanskrit mantras like "Om," considered to be the first sound of the universe, or "So Hum," which translates into "I am that". You can find many more ancient examples online.

Your mantra can also be a single word or phrase in your own language that feels significant. Words like *Love, Peace, Loving Peace, Trust, I am, Yes,* are all acceptable. Sometimes I'll focus on an intention for the day with my mantra, such as *Happy Momentum, Patience, Smile, Listen or Joyous Gratitude.* You can also just hum in your head. Keep it to three words or less. The main purpose of the mantra is to keep you centered and to give you a simple focus to come back to when your mind inevitably wanders… and it will wander. If your thoughts turn to your to-do list, just gently come back, as often as you need to. If your heart leads you to a more "open to receive" place, then let it, and see what comes up. It can be an exciting journey. The more you Go Inside, the less your mind will try to control and the more your heart will open and inspiration will flow.

Peaceful Practice

Even though it's simple, it's not necessarily easy (at first), so don't get discouraged if you struggle to quiet your mind. It took me a lot of practice to get better at not heading into thinking mode so much, and instead learn how to let go and really relax. Going Inside can also bring up uncomfortable feelings or memories. Don't be afraid of that. In fact, embrace the discomfort and just be with it. When you do that, you allow those repressed feelings to be released. It can be a very emotional and cleansing experience. If it feels too intense, remember, you are just sitting. That's all. You are safe. You are just sitting. Stay with it, let go and magic can happen.

After just 31 days straight of Going Inside, I was a changed person. I felt lighter, healthier, happier, and so much more at ease. I was calmer and clearer and better able to handle stress. All of these mental attributes contribute to being a better artist and entrepreneur. I have continued the practice daily and now I actually crave it. Going Inside is basically my daily "happy pill". Often after Going Inside, I'm given new ideas about how to run a better life and business.

Kyle Cease, a professional comic and transformational speaker, gives a great contemporary explanation of how to reap the benefits of a daily meditation practice in this video: http://bit.ly/2psvtfW

Another benefit to Going Inside regularly, will be the ever-growing confidence to trust yourself more. You'll find that you really do have all the answers inside you and you do not need to rely on the outside world for praise or permission. That voice inside all of us is brilliant and all-knowing. We just have to let ourselves get quiet enough to listen to it. How you feel on a daily basis has everything to do with your business success.

Your Time To Go Inside

Feel like you are too busy to Go Inside? Buddhist philosophy rightly claims that, "If you don't have five minutes a day to meditate, then you need an hour!" Think about it. That is so true. If you cannot schedule five minutes for yourself out of a 24-hour day, you absolutely need to adjust your priorities! At what point do we stop and say, "Hey, this is my life and I deserve to be good to myself... every day!"

Go Outside

Another way to combat overwhelm and clear your mind is to go outside. Take a walk. Be in nature if you can. If you live in a city, go to a park. Momma nature is an amazing nurturer. It's that simple.

Part of the reason meditation and communing with nature is so effective is that it is a moment in time when you are giving yourself a gift. You are honoring yourself. If you don't take care of yourself, how can you truly take care of anyone else or give back to the world?

Go Now

Why not give this a try right now? Put the book down and turn off any music and audible notifications on your devices. You can start with just three minutes. You have three minutes, don't you? Set a timer so you don't think about the time. Just sit comfortably, close your eyes, pick a word to repeat silently, and just breathe. Three minutes, that's all. And then tomorrow, do it again.

If happiness paid the bills,
what would you be doing every day?

"DAVE" from *Evolving Out Loud*

WHAT TO SELL

There are basic guidelines as to what you can and cannot sell on Etsy.

What you cannot sell are items that you did not make or design – also called reselling. This applies to everything on their site except the vintage and craft supply categories. In the vintage category, items must be at least 20 years old.

What you can sell is almost everything else handmade.

Here is just a partial list of possibilities:
Paper and party supplies, art and collectables, bath and beauty products, wedding items, books, toys, games, clothing, jewelry, and objects for home and living.

You can also sell some foodstuffs, like candy and homemade baked goods. However, there are strict guidelines for the food items and you'll need to find out what the laws are in your state regarding making, labeling, and selling food online.

Your Creative Gift

What should you sell? Well, if you are a fine artist looking to become an entrepreneur, look at what you do best and then adjust, if needed. Etsy is known as a place to find handcrafted goods, or crafts in particular. Some of it is fine art to, say, be hung on the wall, but the majority of what you'll find and what buyers are looking for are crafts, also known as "art that functions."

If you don't know what you want to make to sell, then I suggest you peruse through Etsy and see what's out there. Start with the medium you're most comfortable with, be it paint or fabric or clay, whatever. When you find shops that speak to you, then you're headed in the right direction. What could you make that is like or *better than* what you see other artists making? The possibilities are endless, but the key to knowing for sure is to follow your heart and that gut feeling when it happens.

The Real Deal

But what are you really selling? That's a

bigger question than you might imagine and here's why. Why do people shop on Etsy, let's say, instead of a large chain store or more commercial sites, like Walmart or Amazon?

People choose Etsy over the other corporate options for a few reasons. It may be that they want to support a small business or an artisan, like you. I believe that the bigger, more compelling reason to shop on Etsy is that they are looking for something special and unique that they can't find anywhere else. They do also want to support the small business entrepreneur. That is why I shop on Etsy.

One of the most visited areas on any website is the "about" page. I once bought a pair of hand-knitted mittens from a mother in Poland. Her "about" picture showed her smiling with a baby on her hip, in a very grey, pre World War II looking kitchen. I felt really good supporting her, all the way from the United States to Poland, and her mittens were awesome. It also made a great story for the recipient of those mittens. This is why your story is so important and will add value to your shop when you set it up.

More Than Just a Thing

Whatever you decide to sell, it's not just an

object to be worn, displayed or drunk out of. In my case, The Quoted Cup is so much more than just clay cups with sayings on them. Yes, they are practical and yes, they are durable and functional. But my customers want something that I made that conveys not just a message (literally), but also a feeling. Perhaps it's love, as in a favorite Shakespearian quote, or poetry for a spouse. Or the message is joy, as in a celebratory quote for a graduation, retirement, or birthday celebration.

I have received beautiful, heart-wrenching thank yous when the perfect quote helped lift the spirits of someone in need. One woman thanked me for the juice cup that stated, "Though she be but little, she is fierce." which she gave to her friend who was undergoing chemotherapy. These are the times when I love running The Quoted Cup the most. To be able to positively affect someone I don't even know is an amazing feeling.

I have been the happy and grateful recipient of hundreds of 5-star reviews from my customers who not only appreciate the quality of what I make, but also how it makes them feel. To give a gift that is handmade, of superb quality and truly one-of-kind is to say that you really care about the person you are giving it to.

Etsy offers us a place where people can shop thoughtfully. As a seller, you can offer that perfect gift solution.

So when you are making your products, think about the person who might receive them. Make your own art of course, the way you want and need to make it, but do it the best way you know how. Always, always, always make quality a priority. You should be proud of your work and know that it is made well and will hold together once it leaves your studio and heads out into the world. Above all, you want to make your customer happy. Good questions to keep in mind are: What problem are you solving? What need are you filling? Why should someone buy your stuff?

Your Customer

Who is your customer? This can be a tricky question. Whatever you do, know that your customer is *not everyone*. That is a common mistake among new business builders. You make something that is unique, and your buyer is also unique. You want to get clear on this so that you are better at describing and marketing your goods. You want your customer to be able to find you, so key words in the description will help with that.

Remember to go back to your Why. Why

are you doing this? What do you seek? Is it freedom, creative outlet, helping others, expanding your community, growing as a person and an artist? When you are clear on your Why you are much more likely to enjoy the process of your business. When you are clear on your Why you are much more likely to stick it out when business is slow or times get tough. I recommend watching the TED Talk by Simon Sinek called "How Great Leaders Inspire Action" at:
http://bit.ly/2qTo21p

When you sell something you make, you are also selling a part of yourself, and that is what makes it interesting. Your particular artistry, your special point of view, the colors and materials you choose – that's the uniqueness people are searching for. So be real, love what you do, and share that with the world. There are multitudes of people out there who are looking for exactly what you have to offer.

You don't have to run faster
than the bear to get away.
You just have to run faster
than the guy next to you.

JIM BUTCHER

HOW TO SELL YOUR STUFF

You only have to be a little bit better than your competition to stand out in your field. Artists and craftspeople have traditionally sold their wares at art fairs, galleries, and retail shops. With Etsy, your retail shop is your online presence and you want to "get people in the door". In a sea of sellers on the web, you need to be resourceful to stand out. There are many ways to do that. First, start with what you know.

Who You Are

Create a strong name for your business and know how to describe it in a few words. I suggest getting a business card made as soon as possible. There are many online sites that offer very inexpensive business card services that also include the design work. I've used Vistaprint.com and have been happy with their prices and results.

The Quoted Cup business card.
Designed by Julia Henzerling www.Henzerling.org

Once you have your card, you have something tangible to actually give to people when they ask you about what you do for a living. This will also help you get comfortable with talking about your work and your shop. It's a good idea to write down and then practice, out loud, your own "elevator pitch." An elevator pitch is a business term that refers to a succinct and persuasive sales pitch that you can deliver in under 30 seconds, the average time spent in an elevator. This is about you being clear on exactly what you do and why it is good. The purpose of the elevator pitch is to quickly inspire the person you are talking to to want to know more.

Here's my elevator pitch:

Hi, I'm Mandy and I run The Quoted Cup. I create unique, high quality, cast ceramic cups with any quote you want fired onto the surface. They are beautiful, durable, and affordable, so they make great gifts, and they are also something you'd want to have for yourself. We make wine cups and coffee and beer mugs. They are slip cast so the forms match to make great sets. But the individual glazing makes each one unique. The Quoted Cup has an existing catalogue of quotes that range from Shakespeare to inspirational but you can also customize your cup with any text, logo, or picture you'd like. I run most of my business through my online shop at Etsy.com. Here's my card.

A good way to get comfy with your pitch is to practice in a mirror or record yourself. The more comfortable you are, the more confident you'll be when you talk about your work. You want your pitch to be concise and to the point. You want to solve a problem for the person (e.g., they need a beautiful, affordable, custom gift). You also want this to be a conversation. Don't forget to listen! Listening is your most valuable tool in any conversation.

Pitch It Online

When you're talking to the online world, it's a similar approach. In this fast-paced world of technology, you have mere seconds to get someone's attention. Your photos and the first words they see are what will either keep them interested or bore them, thus sending them away. Don't be discouraged if your first forays into online marketing turn up little to no response. This sort of thing takes time and you need to practice and try out different methods until you find the ways that work for you.

Etsy is not a quick-fix enterprise. It's a long-term commitment to building a quality business from quality effort and excellent products.

Marketing is Cooler Than You Think

The word "marketing" often sends people, especially artists, into a panic. There is often the fear that you may be "pushing" your work onto people who don't want it, that you're being obnoxious, that you're "selling your soul" or "selling out" by trying to sell your wares. This is simply not true. Marketing is just another way of telling people about what you've got.

There doesn't have to be anything pushy about it. In fact, you probably do marketing all the time for other people and don't even realize it. Have you ever tried a product, liked it, and then told other people about it? That, my friend, is marketing. So when it comes to your own work, talking about it is just sharing information with other people. Also, when people shop on Etsy, they are looking for something special. You are there to provide them with just what they are looking for. They *want* to find you.

You Are Not Your Art

For artists, actively marketing our work can feel terrifying because we often so closely associate who we are with what we make. You are not the art you make. You are a person who makes the art. Period. Your creativity is a gift and you are lucky to have it. Not sharing it with the world denies others of your gift. If no one immediately buys your creation, or even if they outrightly state that they don't like it, this has no bearing on whether you are a worthy artist or a worthy person. Of course you are worthy and you are on this earth for a reason!

Your value is not about the value placed on your art. Your job as an artist is to make your work and share it with the world. If you can make money from your creative talents, even better. But money is not necessary to justify the making of, or establishing the real value of art. Take a look at this interview between Marie Forleo and Elizabeth Gilbert: http://bit.ly/2pZxUYd

For every creative person, I highly recommend reading Liz's book, *Big Magic*.

We live in a world where having money is essential to create the lifestyle we want, so you will need to be making it somewhere. Making money from your creativity is just as valid as making it from any other source. This is an important distinction that you need to really understand, deep inside you, at a cellular level.

The Quoted Cup is a way for me to continue working in my studio, but on a commercial platform. I create a distinction between my fine art and my commercial art because that is what works for me. I love my production cup business and this part of my creative self. My commercial art is also my bread and butter in the studio. This frees me up to not think about money when it comes to my fine art, and therefore, in that arena, I can focus solely on the creative process and what pleases me, and me alone.

Tell Everybody

Once your shop is up, start sending out images and simple text about your work on social media. There are many options, from Facebook, Instagram, Pinterest, Twitter, and more. Start with what you already know and are most comfortable with. You can expand your knowledge of other outlets later or hire someone to do that for you.

Post regularly and start building a following. You want people to repost your images, head to your shop, and of course, buy your work. If you don't know how to do this, just ask. There are many people who spend a lot of time online and understand almost everything when it comes to the Internet, especially when it comes to social media. There are also marketing companies that you can hire to showcase your work on the web. Do your research on them and ask for examples of how they operate.

Your Purple Cow

Think about what makes your work and

your shop stand out above all others. What is your purple cow? That is a reference to Seth Godin's business guidebook, *Purple Cow: Transform Your Business by Being Remarkable*. This is a unique business book. It helps you to focus on what makes your business special in the sea of businesses online. Your "purple cow" could be anything from the remarkable product you make to the exceptional customer service you provide, or both.

Etsy also offers advice in the area of marketing. They want you to be a successful seller because it benefits them as well. There are many helpful articles posted in the *Seller Handbook* section of the site. They cover topics like Getting Found, Productivity, and Branding and Marketing. These articles along with the teams and forum discussions are great resources for your journey to becoming a successful entrepreneur.

Choose Wisely

Whatever methods you utilize to market your work, it's most important to keep focusing on your goals, not the obstacles. Certainly *learn* from the obstacles, but then move on. If something doesn't work, try something else, again and again and again if need be. Remember, this is business. It's not personal. It is normal for it to take some time for a business to start making money, that's ok. This is a learning curve, and the more time you spend learning how to run your business, the better you'll get. Allow your work and your process to evolve when it needs to. The more open you are to learning how to do this, the more success you will have.

To order space is to give it meaning.

ISAMU NOGUCHI

YOUR SPACE

The space you work in says a lot about the business you run. While you don't have to be a total neat-nick, a sloppy, disorganized workspace will hinder your work process and affect your business negatively. Organization is a key element to a successful business of any kind. You don't want to waste your time looking for things in your own work environment. Honoring your space by keeping it organized is a way to honor yourself and your business. If this does not come naturally to you, know that it is something you can learn.

If you are working out of the space you live in or just a very small space, get yourself some plastic bins to help keep you organized. Separate the bins into each "room" of your shop: Photography, Shipping, Orders, Supplies, Office, etc. The kitchen table can be all spaces in one if need be, as long as you can find what you need when you need it.

Your Office Space

Your office serves as the place where you figure out how to make your business successful. Your office is also where the money comes in and goes out, so it's essential to your business.

I suggest you have a cabinet or filing boxes to make file categories like Sales, Taxes, Supplies, Receipts, Shipping, Orders, etc. Some of these files can be on your virtual desktop. That's fine, as long as you can keep them organized and up to date.

Your Making Space

Your workspace can be a separate studio or just the kitchen table. It doesn't matter as long as it works for you. Again, stay as organized as you can, as this will reduce interruptions and enhance the creative flow. Using separate bins or shelves for supplies, tools and finished products is a must. Good lighting is also important.

Since you probably have another job to make your money, you'll need to make your crafts on your down time. You'll have to find time to make the work. Don't quit your day job until you're sure that your business is sustainable. Make time to do your work by scheduling it on the calendar and sticking to it. Know what your goals and your desired outcomes are before you sit down to create. Allow flexibility, but have goals in mind. The making is the good part and you want to enjoy it and make the most out of it!

Your Photography Space

Find an area where you can easily set up for a photo session. Using natural light from a nearby window tends to be best. You can also rely on separate lighting. Details on this are covered in the Photography section of this book. What's most important is that you plan a space for taking great pictures that you can easily setup and breakdown.

Your Shipping Space

You'll need a place to wrap and pack your orders up. Have your tape, labels, and boxes always stocked so that you are ready to ship. The "handling" part of Shipping and Handling refers to the materials you use and the time it takes to pack up an order. This can be surprisingly inefficient and costly if you don't have a system in place. More on this is covered in the shipping section of this book.

The people that succeed
are the people who don't quit.

CYNDI LAUPER

TAKING CARE OF BUSINESS

Paperwork

Paperwork is a necessary part of any business, but it does not have to be depressing. To avoid feeling overwhelmed or frustrated, block out short, specific times when you will focus only on the paperwork. You'll be more efficient and happier if you group your tasks into manageable time blocks, say an hour or two at a time. Put it on your calendar and stick to it. Instead of dreading it, see it as essential to your success. When you sit down to tackle the paperwork, value your time by eliminating any distractions, such as email, social media, and telephone interruptions.

Most artists that I know, including myself, don't like to deal with paperwork. It is a very left-brained activity and creatives are generally right-brained people. However, paperwork should not be seen as a chore, but rather, as the bones of your business. Make the entire processes "part of your art" and don't emotionally separate tasks. Each element is inclusive to your success, so give your love to *all* of it!

Accounting

Once you get going on Etsy and make your first sale, you are a business! If you make more than $600 annually, you'll need to know how to pay your taxes. If you don't already have an accountant, I suggest you at least consult with one or meet with a bookkeeper to get an overview of what you need to pay attention to and keep track of.

I am not an accountant and am not licensed to dispense financial advice. The notes in this chapter are just some of the current United States tax requirements that I am aware of. Again, please seek the advice of a financial professional for your business.

Self-employment income requires that you file a Schedule C "Profit or Loss from Business". If you make more than $20,000 annually, Etsy will issue you a 1099k, which will be reported to the IRS. But even if you make less, as a sole proprietor, you are required to pay your taxes quarterly or biannually. This means that every three or six months you pay taxes on the sales you've earned so far. Or you file and say that you made no money, if that is the case. This actually will make your life easier when tax time rolls around, as you will have already done the legwork and paid upfront. You can track your Etsy earnings easily in the Shop Stats section of your shop. The Etsy *Seller Handbook* also offers a free guide called *Taxes 101 For Etsy Sellers*.

Hiring an accountant or bookkeeper will aid in you having more time to do what you're good at – creating! You can often find free or low cost business financial advice at your local small business development center. The IRS also offers free tax advice and services. Remember, just because you *can* do something, doesn't mean you should! It took me years to finally hire a bookkeeper and I only wish I had done it sooner! When I was doing my own books, it was detrimental to my creative process and it took a lot of time, and I hated it. Once I buckled down and hired a bookkeeper, no surprise, my sales went up and paid for the bookkeeper!

When you let go of feeling like you have to

do everything and instead only do what you are good at, magic happens. So ask yourself what your time is worth and where you are best at spending it.

Building Your List

An important category to any online business is your list. Your list is an ongoing record, specifically names and email addresses, of current and potential customers. If people have inquired, they have expressed interest, and you want to be able to communicate with them when you have new products, services or sales. Make a habit of collecting people's contact information and keeping it updated. If someone sends you a question about your product, be sure to stop and put their info into a web list or digital address book with any notes about them, like what products they asked about or purchased and when. This is extremely important as you grow your business.

Use this information, respectfully, to stay in contact with people about what you are doing. Your best customer is your repeat customer. There are many online list and email marketing services like MailChimp, AWeber, and Emma that you can use to store and utilize your contact information effectively. Be sure that your list contacts know that they can unsubscribe at any time. You can easily start your list with the existing digital address book on your computer desktop. Make a separate folder to designate them as your business list. Your list is your people!

Your Most Valuable Resource

Your time is the one resource you cannot get back, so use it efficiently, especially when you are doing things you don't really enjoy doing. I recommend the YouTube video excerpt from Tony Robbins called *Take Immediate Control of Your Day and 10X Your Productivity* at: http://bit.ly/2qTFfrH

In the video, he coaches a roomful of corporate salespeople about outcome-focused thinking and he also works directly with a woman to understand the value of paperwork. You'll find this specific interaction at 50:35. It's inspiring and worth the watch. Tony illustrates how when you change the language around your tasks, you change the meaning of the task altogether. He also illustrates how when you focus on your desired outcome, instead of your tasks, you naturally come up with better ways to get the job done. As I mentioned earlier, this focused thinking is a much more efficient and successful way to go about any situation, be it business or personal. Once I incorporated this method into my daily life, everything got easier.

The price of anything
is the amount of life you exchange for it.

HENRY DAVID THOREAU

PRICING YOUR WORK

While the work you produce from your
personal artistry and style may have started as
a labor of love, your Etsy shop is a business.
A business needs to make money to survive,
period. There are many factors that can go
into how much you should charge for your
products. You need to consider not only the
cost of raw materials, but also the time you
spent making the work. This can include time
spent designing, sourcing materials, actual
production, photographing, tending to your
shop, and shipping and handling.

When you first get started, you may not be
able to charge what you want based on how
much time you've invested, because start-up
costs are just that – the costs of getting
started. But once you are on a roll, pay
attention to and write down how much time

you spend doing specific tasks. Figure out how much you want to make per hour. Also, alter that hourly rate based on the task. You wouldn't make as much per hour shipping orders as you would designing or fabricating your products. Then balance these factors with what the market will bear. See what else is out there in your field and price your work in a way that represents the quality of your work and the profile of your customer. If you make a better product, you can charge more for it.

Your Customer

Who is your customer? This is an important question to know the answer to. The first thing you need to understand is that YOU are NOT your customer. That's right, you are not making this for you, you are making it for someone else. Someone else who may likely be in a different tax bracket! So don't ask yourself what you *would* or worse, *could* afford to pay for your own item. What is considered "affordable" is an abstract idea that is different for everyone. This is especially important if you come from any kind of "starving artist" concept of yourself. There are plenty of people out there who make more money than you and are happy to spend it on quality goods.

Something perceived as priced too low, will often be seen as not valuable at all. One of the advantages an independent, creative business has over the big-box, corporate retailers is the personal touch, the attention to detail, and the originality. Often, people who are shopping on Etsy expect to pay more because they want something handmade, something different, and something special. That is what you are offering.

Find Your Customer

You can find your ideal customer by understanding your target market and defining your niche market. Your target market is a group of potential customers who share qualities related to your product. For example, literary people, Shakespeare enthusiasts, and fans of inspirational quotes are my target audience.

A niche market is more defined. My niche market for The Quoted Cup is male and female, discerning gift givers who favor quality over quantity, and they are looking for a unique and handmade functional art. My customer wants something practical but original, and they care what they eat and drink out of and how their dinner table looks. My customer does not mind paying more for a quality product, in fact, they expect to. My customer would not buy a typical mass-produced ceramic coffee cup from a big-box chain store. I make it a point to cater my goods to my customers and constantly strive to improve my line to give them what they want.

Doing The Math

How much to charge for your work is variable.

There are numerous ways to calculate your prices but here is one basic formula from the Etsy *Seller Handbook*:

(Hourly Overhead + Production Costs + Profit) x 4 = Retail Price

Your hourly overhead is your business expenses (from utilities to rent) over 12 months, divided by the hours you work on your business.

Your production costs are your (hourly wage x hours creating the piece) + materials cost.

Your profit is the markup you charge to grow your business. The markup on raw materials is typically 100% or double the original price. I add up the cost of my raw cups, plus glaze, plus decals, plus firing costs, plus employees, plus the time it takes to make it all from start to finish. This leaves me with a reliable base price from which to mark up to a fair retail price for the product.

Your work, education, and art experience can also be a factor in the price you charge. The more knowledgeable and educated you are in your field, the more your skills are worth. When you are just starting out, pricing can be a tough hurdle to jump. It's important to take the emotion out of the equation and replace it with math. In fact, creating a spreadsheet with your formula for pricing is a great way to let go and learn how to charge what it's really worth.

Again, remember, it's not personal. It's business. When just starting out, before you have 12 months of numbers, take into account what the market in your field supports. Find items like yours and get a sense of what people are paying for them. Sometimes it's good to start out charging a little less to entice people into your shop. Measure their responses and go from there.

Just Do It

Once you've found your price point, finish your listing and publish it. And then, be patient. Don't get upset if nothing happens in a week or even a month. Etsy is a huge marketplace and it takes time to create a presence. If after a month and lots of views there are no sales, it's easy to go back into your listing and adjust the price, as well as photos and listing text if desired.

It won't cost you any money to edit your listings.

When you look at other sellers' prices for items that are similar to yours, you shouldn't copy what someone else does, or price yourself out the market, but you do want to get the right amount for the value you provide. If this all seems overwhelming at first, don't worry, it gets easier. You can find more tips and some in-depth articles on pricing and finding your ideal customer in the Etsy *Seller Handbook*. Running a business is always about learning and growing. It's an investment of not only money, but time, and it can be well worth it.

Nothing wrong with making money.

ADAM LEVINE

MAKING MONEY

You are in business to make money. That is what it's all about. While money can't buy you happiness or love, it is a necessary tool to function well in our modern world. And a tool is just what it is. It's something we use to get what we want. But like politics and religion, money is a hot topic that triggers people strongly in one way or another. The fact that you're reading this book says that you are interested in making some money, preferably from your creative endeavors.

I have found that money can be an especially awkward topic for artists. This is probably due to how much we associate ourselves with the work that we produce. This can be a tricky psychological minefield. While it's true that your work comes from you and you alone, it is not you. It is your work. Being creative is a gift and it's your mission, if you choose to accept it, to share it with the world. You are luckier than most, to have this creative gift, but it's not your baby, it's your work! So make sure that you can step back and understand this.

Elizabeth Gilbert offers a wonderful and thought provoking angle on this thing we call creativity in her TED Talk entitled "Your Elusive Creative Genius" at: http://bit.ly/2pUnhrJ

Your Money Issues

It is important to get clear on your issues with money and how it makes you feel. Your goal is to feel good about making money from your work, period. If you are in any way not comfortable with the subject of money and specifically you making it, I urge you to look deeper into why, because otherwise this will negatively affect your experience and success in business. For example, if you think that people who have money are bad people, guess what, your subconscious will protect you by not letting you make any money. Seriously.

I use a few key questions about emotions around money in my Worksheet #4: MY MONEY, but I do recommend this read by Kate Northrup, as she speaks directly to the subject in depth of emotional blocks around money, in her book *Money: A Love Story*.

There are many more resources online that can assist you in this area. I recommend seeking out experts on money like Tony Robbins, Robert Kiyosaki, Marie Forleo, Barbara Stanny and Napoleon Hill, just to name a few. Search them out and follow up on the resources that speak to you the most.

How much money do you want to make? In a day, in a month, or in a year? Clarity is key. Knowing how much you want to make keeps you more focused on how much you need to be putting into your business. Keep a journal and write down your financial goals. When your goals change, write them down. Get clear and comfortable with the money subject and you'll find that the flow of money will get comfy with you. When it comes to money, you can't be too educated or too inspired!

Download Worksheet #4: MY Money at:
www.FromArtisticToEntrepreneur.com

MY MONEY

MY BELIEFS ABOUT MONEY AND MY MONEY GOALS

WORKSHEET #4

 If happiness paid the bills, I'd be making a living...

 I think money is:

 People who make a lot of money are:

 How do I *want* to feel about money?

 How much money do I *need* to make annually?

    This breaks down to a monthly income of:

    This breaks down to a weekly income of:

 How much money do I *want* to make annually?

    This breaks down to a monthly income of:

    This breaks down to a weekly income of:

 Here are some ways I can use my creativity to make the money I *want* to make:

81

When the Money Comes

One of my favorite parts of Etsy is how easy they make it to safely collect money from your sales through their Seller Protected options. In Payment Settings, you'll enter your own bank account where you want funds to be deposited. Etsy accepts all the major credit cards and they handle the transactions. After subtracting their 3.5% fee, the funds are deposited into your Etsy Shop Payment Account to then be transferred to your designated checking account whenever you schedule it.

Another option for accepted payments is through PayPal inside or outside of Etsy. You set your PayPal account up directly on the PayPal site. You can either choose to manually move your funds from PayPal to your bank account or you can set Etsy up to direct deposit PayPal sales into your Etsy Shop Payment Account.

In your Shop Payment Account, you'll also enter your debit card or a credit card that can be used to pay the monthly tally of listing fees and promotions you may have purchased. Etsy will email you an invoice monthly and you can choose to manually pay it or set up automatic payments.

What Is Selling and What Is Not Selling

When you get your monthly statement, it's a good idea to understand exactly where the fees came from. You can research every sale you've ever made via the Order Activity list and see not only what sold, but how much you paid per item to Etsy. The more you understand your sales, the better you'll be at pricing your work and feeling comfortable about it all.

Etsy is very good at providing stats (statistics), and stats are a very good source of information about your business. Head on over to the Dashboard page and you can see a breakdown of how many people have visited your shop, favorited your items, and made purchases. This information can be reviewed on a daily, monthly or yearly basis. I like to check in weekly to see not only what is selling but also what cups of mine people are favoriting.

You can track your income in the same way on the Shop Stats page. They provide graphs of all your sales, including a map that gives you a global overview of where you sell. On your Shop Manager page you can see a breakdown of your traffic sources, or how people found you. This will give you insight as to how your social media marketing is working for you. The most searched keywords, most active listings, and the most favorited listings are here as well.

Cha-Ching!

By far, the best designed and most fun Etsy feature is the smartphone app. Every time you make a sale, your phone makes the sound of an old fashioned cash register! That "cha-ching" will put a smile on your face every time, as it audibly signals to you that someone just gave you money for work that you made. Making money is fun! You can also set up your Etsy app to audibly alert you when people favorite your items or shop, have conversations, etc.

When you do start making sales, be ready for it. If you are a business that will be busy in the gift buying seasons, like Christmas, get ready to buckle down and do the work. Hire help if you need to. You can sleep in January.

*A picture
is worth a thousand words.*

ENGLISH IDIOM

PHOTOGRAPHY

The pictures you take are going to be one of the most important aspects of your Etsy shop. It doesn't matter how good your product is, if your pictures are poor, your products won't sell. While this may seem like a daunting thought to some, the photography aspect doesn't have to be difficult. Unlike in the "old days" when you needed a single-lens reflex camera and expensive lighting and real film, you can now shoot great shots with just your cell phone and a little ingenuity.

First off, decide where your "photo studio" will be. Is it inside or out? Does that space change? A good way to help you decide on that space is to look at the photographs from other people's shops. Search items that are similar to yours and make notes on the shops whose pictures draw you in, make you want to click and see more.

Your first photo of the ten you can have will be the photo that shows up in all postings, like Facebook, Twitter, and Instagram. You want that photo to stand out and be the best one to attract more attention and invite the viewer to look at more of your work. Eye-catching shots are often attained by using an interesting close-up or detail shot as the first photo. When you are looking at the photos from other shops, also make notes about the pictures you do not like. Why don't you like them? Is it the lighting, the space, or is it too cluttered with many other things in the shot? Is the object for sale obvious or are you not sure what you are looking at or what the item is that they are advertising? Scrutinizing other people's photos is a great learning tool.

Your Photo Speaks

When it comes to photography, what you see is literally what you get. So be clear on the message you are sending with the photo of your product. Often, having the item in use is a very good way to sell it. We tend to take for granted what our products are good for and assume everyone will figure that out. Not so! You need to tell an obvious and simple story with your pictures. This is my product, this is what it does, and this is how you can use it. It's imperative that there is no misunderstanding what you are selling. You may want to share your photos with a trusted outside source for feedback before you post them.

Depending on the product you make, it's always a good idea to show the piece in its natural environment. You want to literally show people how your product looks in everyday settings – actually spell it out for them. After many years of doing this, if there is one thing I've learned, it's that people cannot often envision anything past what's right in front of them! When I spell it out for them, in pictures and in words, I make more sales.

Size Matters

You also want the photo to give the piece a sense of scale, so it's obvious to the viewer how big or small it is. For example, if you are shooting jewelry, take numerous types of shots. You want at least one close-up on a white background. You also want a shot with the jewelry being worn or even held, so people can understand it's size and how it looks against skin or clothing. You might try using props or everyday items next to the piece, like a wine glass or keys. Even though a cup or a mug is pretty easy to guess in size, in some of my shots I include props like books or a wine bottle. I also use wedding rings to illustrate the beauty and meaning of the Lover's Cups.

The Lover's Cups with props.

Where to Shoot

If you are shooting your work inside, then find a place that can either be left alone to be ready at any time for a photo shoot, or can easily be set up at a moment's notice for a rapid shoot. This is important, as you want to get your new photos or new listings up as quickly as possible once your product is ready for sale. It's also a good idea to shoot several pieces at once to be efficient with your time.

For lighting you want to use "white" light, either fluorescent or Cool White LED (not Warm White). You do not want a typical incandescent house light bulb, which produces a warm/yellow effect. You can buy workshop clip-on lights at any hardware store or online. Once you've picked your light fixtures, you'll want to diffuse the light. Diffusing means you soften the light of the bulb, which softens the light on the work so it's not so harsh. You can carefully tape tracing paper across the shade, in front of the bulb, but be wary of the possible fire hazard – bulbs can get very hot! You can also find inexpensive photo set ups and diffusers online. What I use is a kit that contains two light stands, complete with fluorescent bulbs and diffuser umbrellas.

This kit is affordable and easy to set up and put away. The white umbrella in front of the bulbs diffuses the light beautifully. Though you typically would not necessarily have light behind your subject, I make it work in my photos. You can find my preferred light kit setup at: www.FromArtisticToEntrepreneur.com

How To Shoot

You'll want light to come from two different angles, so as not to create really sharp shadows. For my cups, I typically have one light shining midway on the piece from the left and front angle. The right light shines from above and in front of the work. Once I look through the lens, I adjust the light specifically to what looks best. Again, what you see through the lens is what you'll get. There are also pre-made light boxes available for mostly smaller objects, which make shooting very easy and well lit. Whatever you do, do NOT use a flash when taking pictures of your work.

My camera is on a tripod to keep it steady and I highly recommend that you use a tripod, even if you're shooting with a cell phone. You can find inexpensive tripods of many styles and sizes online. If you are photographing a number of pieces at one time, put them in groups of similar size and shape. You'll want to have the camera and lighting setup so that you can easily and quickly take numerous shots in a row. In other words, make it a production line of pictures by shooting all the same size objects one after the other, then resetting your camera angle to shoot all of the detail shots in a row, etc. This approach will make your photo sessions go much faster.

Check your work on a computer screen as you go. I use a digital single lens reflex (DSLR) camera and I regularly pop out the memory card and put it in my laptop to see the shots in a larger format. You can do this with a cell phone too, by plugging it into a computer and opening the photo editing software you've chosen. This is important, as you'll see where things aren't working, like if it's too dark, or there's dirt on the table you didn't notice, or there's something in the background that you don't want in the shot. You want to be sure you like the direction you are going *before* you break down your photo setup!

When To Shoot

If you're shooting your work outdoors, or even near a window, as I do, you'll need to keep in mind the time of day and type of day that works best. A bright, sunny day does not provide the best light to shoot in, as it creates harsh light and strong shadows. Slightly overcast daylight, or a cloudy day is actually what will give you the best overall light. Photographing outside means you'll need to schedule your photo sessions around Mother Nature, which can be tricky.

In my case, I shoot indoors but by a south-facing window. I know that I need to shoot in the morning or in the late afternoon, when the sun is on either side of my tabletop and not shining right on it and creating shadows. I also do a tricky shoot with my work being in front of a window, meaning light is coming from behind, which in general is a big no-no. But I make it work by correctly lighting the front of my piece from two sides and creating a shallow depth of field that makes the background blur away.

My standard photography spot with lights and camera on tripods.

I then do some adjusting in my image editing program to brighten the cups in the foreground, crop the picture, and straighten it out if needed. The next two images are the same photograph, before and after editing.

The original, un-edited photograph.

The final edited photograph – straightened, cropped and lightened.

A shallow depth of field means that the foreground object is in focus but the background is not. This is a great way to make your one object stand out. If you are using a camera that allows you to adjust the aperture, or width opening of the lens, remember that the bigger the number, the more things that are in focus. For example, an aperture of 11 will have more things in focus than an aperture of 5.6.

Another background option for shooting your work is to use a seamless backdrop. This consists of a long piece of paper that seamlessly flows down from the wall behind the object towards the camera. It creates a background that disappears and seems infinite. It also makes the object the only image in the photograph, without any background distractions.

There are specific photography light box kits with built-in seamless backdrops that make shooting smaller work very easy. I've listed a popular one on my resources page: www.FromArtisticToEntrepreneur.com

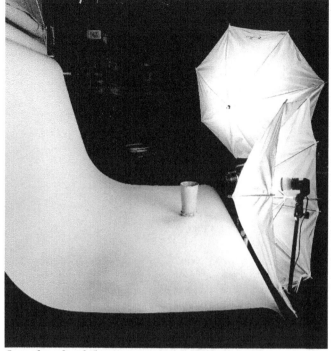

Seamless backdrop set-up with diffused lights, camera and cup. This can also be achieved on a smaller scale.

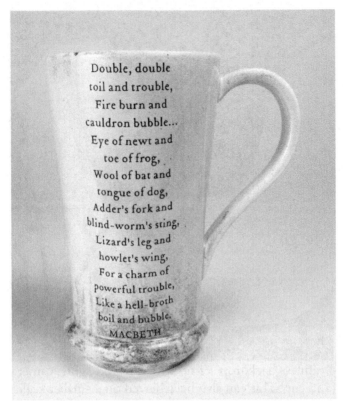

Cup photographed with seamless backdrop.

You'll develop the photographic style that is right for you by experimenting. My cups along with my photography skills have come a long way since I first started my Etsy business.

2011: One of the first wheel thrown Shakespeare mugs, photographed in my kiln shed.

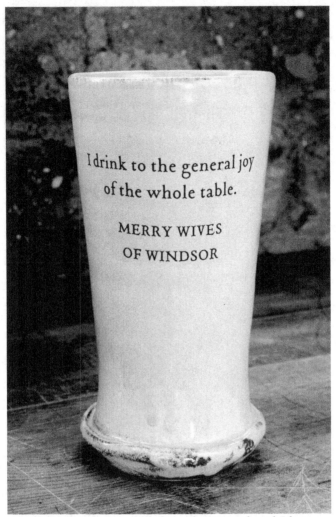

I drink to the general joy of the whole table.

MERRY WIVES OF WINDSOR

2012: My pottery skills have improved and I have established a standard shape for my beer mugs. I am still shooting in my kiln shed.

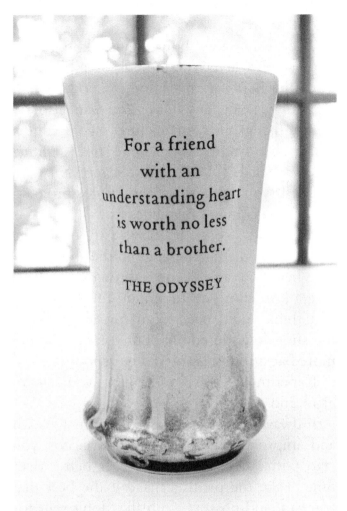

For a friend
with an
understanding heart
is worth no less
than a brother.

THE ODYSSEY

2017: My cup designs are now slip cast for uniformity and production efficiency, to keep up with increasing orders. My photography spot has moved to a brighter place.

Shoot Away!

The great thing about digital photography is that you can take hundreds of pictures to learn the best way to shoot your own work, without wasting any film. You can also do major fixing of your pictures with editing software. There are even free editing programs like GIMP, PhotoScape, Nik and Pixler. If you use a MAC, the Photos program has simple editing capabilities as well, which is what I use. You can play with exposure, cropping, and straightening out the shot.

When you are looking through the lens, give a little more room around the piece than you think you'll need. You can always crop the shot down in editing, but you cannot add more background if you did not shoot it.

Experiment, play, and allow yourself to grow and adapt over time.

I always know that there is room to learn and improve. No matter what photos you start with, they will naturally get better over time. Take the picture, make it the best that you can, and post it. No really, don't wait for it to be perfect and don't hesitate to get it up there on your listing! You can always go back later and update the photos. It's a good idea to check back in and create new photos from time to time if you need to anyway. It keeps your site fresh and interesting.

*We can't become
what we can't envision.*

MARIE FORLEO

SETTING UP YOUR SHOP

Setting up your shop on Etsy is a fairly easy process, but it can be a time consuming one, at first. Before you sign on to begin the setup, be prepared. If you have your basic information at your fingertips, it will go quicker and you'll have more fun.

Here's a list of what you'll need to get started to open your Etsy shop:

I've created an easy to follow Set-Up Checklist Worksheet for what you'll need to have ready to open your shop.

Download Worksheet #5: MY SHOP at:
www.FromArtisticToEntrepreneur.com

MY SHOP OPENING LIST

💡 **My 40 FREE LISTINGS:** www.FromArtisticToEntrepreneur.com

💡 **My User Name:** This is my sign-in name, only visible to me. I cannot change it once I open my shop.

💡 **My Password:** This is a password I can remember. I'll need it online and for the app.

💡 **My Shop Name:** Here are a few options that I will search online first then I'll search on Etsy. I can change this name as many times as I want BEFORE I open my shop. But as soon as I am open for business, I can only change it *one more time*. Etsy will display my shop name all as one word, though I can put in capital letters to make it more readable.

💡 **My Public Profile Name:** This is visible on my opening page. I can have spaces and use capital letters to delineate between words. I can change this at anytime. This is also where I can use a pen name if I want my personal identity to remain private.

LISTING TIPS

💡 **SEO:** When titling and describing my items, these are words that shoppers would use if they were searching for my product.

MY SHOP
WHAT I NEED TO HAVE READY TO OPEN MY SHOP

 My Items to list: I can open with just one, but at least three items looks better. For each item I have an already written description, the quantity available the price, the processing time and the 13 descriptive tags figured out. I've also figured out the shipping costs or I am using the Calculated Shipping Option.

1.   2.   3.   4.

 My Photos: My images are available and easy to pull from my computer desktop or other folder. Etsy requires that no one dimension is over 1500 pixels.

Item: _____	Item: _____	Item: _____	Item: _____
1.	1.	1.	1.
2.	2.	2.	2.
3.	3.	3.	3.
4.	4.	4.	4.
5.	5.	5.	5.

 My Shipping Options: I can choose calculated shipping, which means each buyer pays the actual amount to their location from mine, calculated by Etsy at checkout.
OR:
This is my Pre-determined shipping price per item:

My shipping cost of extra item in the same order:

My handling charge (if any):

 My Billing Information: Etsy will bill me at the end of each month for any fees.

My Credit or Debit Card #:
Name on Credit Card:
Billing Address:

My Bank Information: This is where I want my money to be sent.
Bank Name:
Account #:
Routing #:

Free Listings:

Use this link to get your first 40 listings for free: www.FromArtisticToEntrepreneur.com

User Name: This is your sign in name, only visible to you and you cannot change it once you open your shop.

Password: This is self-explanatory but pick something you can remember. Etsy has a Seller App and you want to be able to access your shop easily so that you can communicate with customers when needed, and you'll want to hear that "cha-ching!" loud and clear!

Shop Name: Have a few ideas on hand. You never know what might already be taken. Google it and search for it on Etsy. You can change this name as many times as you want BEFORE you click the button to open your shop. But once you are open for business, you can only change it *once*, so feel good about the name you pick.

Etsy will have you write your shop name all as one word, though you can put in capital letters to make it more readable. For example, my shop name when you see it on Etsy is, TheQuotedCup with no spaces between the words. If your desired shop name is taken, try personalizing it with your name, like MandysQuotedCup, or add the word 'shop' or 'boutique' at the end. My shop began as TaosGargirl, but after a few years, when the cups became the main focus, I changed it to TheQuotedCup. I'm happy with that and that is where it will stay.

Public Profile Name: This is visible on your opening page. You can have spaces and use capital letters to delineate between words. You can change this at anytime. This is also where you can use a pen name if you want your personal identity to remain private.

Listing Tips

SEO: This stands for Search Engine Optimization and understanding it is key to getting people to your shop. Done well, it is a process that helps improve the visibility of your shop in search engine results for sites like Bing, Yahoo, and Google. When titling and describing your items, use words that shoppers would use if they were searching for your product. For example, on one of my most popular listings I title it this way: "Mug: Double, Double, Toil and Trouble... Shakespeare's MacBeth's Witches Brew." The title not only describes the item, but uses words a shopper might use to find this type of literary messaged cup.

Items to list: You can open with just one, but I recommend starting with at least three items, so your shop looks fuller. The listing process is easy, but it takes some time at first. Etsy will walk you through it. You'll want to be prepared to enter a description of your work, the price, the quantity you have in stock, your processing time for shipping, and the tags you'll use (more words that buyers would search to find your item).

Photos: Have your finished images available and easy to pull from your computer desktop or other folder. Etsy requires that no one dimension is over 1,500 pixels.

Shipping Information: Etsy uses the US Postal Service and FedEx. You can choose calculated shipping, which means each buyer pays the actual amount to their location from yours, calculated by Etsy at checkout. This is a good option because it makes it fair and easy for you and your buyers. You don't need to make money on the actual shipping and it's already expensive, so I don't recommend that.

You do have the option of entering a "handling" charge, which the buyer won't see but it's added to their calculated shipping costs.

The only problem I've found with calculated shipping is if the buyer orders more than one of my items, there is no way to combine items into a single shipment and reduce the cost. You could get around this by stating something in your listing about manually crediting their order by a percentage or specific amount if they buy multiple items.

The Quoted Cup uses a pre-determined shipping price. I do this because people often order multiple cups and I have a reduced shipping price for two or more items. I figured out a standard price for shipping my products from the east coast to the west that evens out over short and long distances. I've done the same for shipments to other countries.

Your billing information: You'll need a valid credit or debit card to get started. Etsy will bill you at the end of each month.

The Fun Is Just Beginning

The above information is all you need to immediately open your shop and start selling your beautiful wares to the world! It's simple, really. But ultimately you will want to do more. You can continually update and add to your information and have as many listings as you want to.

Head on over the Shop Manager page and click on Settings and you'll see a list of different aspects of your shop. This is a great way to familiarize yourself with all of the options you have to customize your shop. Click on each title and you'll be led through questions that will further complete your profile.

The Pattern Option

You'll see this heading on the left too. Pattern is Etsy's option to turn your Etsy shop into a website that appears to be outside of the Etsy site. It is a .com address that is based on your Etsy shop, but looks different. It's easy to set up and you can customize it. Everything you do on your Etsy site is reflected in your Pattern site, like changing listings, prices, etc. Orders are fulfilled directly from the Pattern site. The funds are handled through Etsy as usual. The cost of the site is $15 per month plus 3.5% in addition to payment processing fees. It is open to sellers who have Direct Checkout enabled, which I recommend. I don't, however, recommend the Pattern site. I found that I didn't get any extra business, only extra fees. There's more detail on the up and down sides of Pattern that you can search for on the web. You need to decide if it's right for you. It's certainly not necessary to have it when you are just starting out. Also, in April of 2017, Etsy made it possible for buyers to checkout without signing up as a member.

About Your Shop

In Shop Settings, the links will take you to pages where you can tell your story and share pictures and even video of who you are and what you do. People love this information. Remember, they are not just buying your work, they are buying "you" and who you are and the story you tell. Have fun with this! If it takes you a while to get these pages complete, that's ok. You can change the information here at any time. This is another place where reading other sellers' profiles and stories can help you create your story. The important thing is that you get your shop opened as soon as possible and go from there. I'm constantly updating and modifying my information since I opened my shop in 2009.

Use the Set-Up Checklist in Worksheet #5 found at:

www.FromArtisticToEntrepreneur.com to get started and then sign on and open up your Etsy shop! Just starting this process will propel you forward. You'll not only have new presence in the online world of commerce, but you'll be able to use Etsy as a tool to learn about business. The forums and the *Etsy Seller Handbook* are full of useful information from and for artists just like you.

And always remember, done is better than perfect! So let's get started!

Mail your packages early
so the post office
can lose them
in time for Christmas.

ROBIN WILLIAMS

SHIPPING

Once you set up your shop with good photographs and descriptions and all your items are priced, be sure that you are ready to ship the item in the time frame you've stated after an order is placed. Make sure you have all of your shipping materials at hand and can quickly fill the orders you get. I've included a Shipping Supplies Worksheet with a list of the basic shipping items you'll want to have at the ready.

Download Worksheet # 6:
MY SHIPPING at:
www.FromArtisticToEntrepreneur.com

MY SHIPPING

MY LIST OF SHIPPING SUPPLIES TO KEEP IN STOCK

WORKSHEET #6

BASIC SHIPPING SUPPLIES: Below are links to recommended products.

2 Inch Wide Packing Tape:
Clear – To secure box and go over label: http://amzn.to/2s81YBA
Brown – To secure box if you like brown tape: http://amzn.to/2qvGY6G

2 Inch Wide Tape Gun:
http://amzn.to/2s89CvU

Boxes: I order the sizes I need from Uline:
https://www.uline.com/Cls_04/Boxes-Corrugated

Stickers or Stamps: Fragile if you need that. Your personal return label with your logo.
http://amzn.to/2rPGLzk

Bubble Wrap: You may want to shop locally for bubble wrap since it is a large item to ship.
3/16th Inch is your small bubble, perforated every 12 inches: http://amzn.to/2qvVbAv
1/2 Inch is the standard 'big' bubble, perforated every 12 inches: http://amzn.to/2sfjdjQ

Packing Peanuts: I recommend that you find recycled ones locally or buy the biodegradable ones! Styrofoam is planetary nightmare. This is also a very large item to ship, so picking it up locally if you can, makes the most sense.
http://amzn.to/2qtFj5M

Colored Tissue Paper: This is an easy and inexpensive way to make my packed products look great.
12" x 18": http://amzn.to/2s84VCe
20" x 26": http://amzn.to/2rPjYU4

Care Instructions: If my item needs any information about cleaning or maintaining its appearance.

Surprise Token Gift: This is not at all necessary but it is a nice gesture – only do this if it's easy; candy or a small object from my work process.

Cloth Grocery Bags: These are very helpful to transport my goods to the P.O. or shipping center.
Medium: http://amzn.to/2ryOpOR
Large: http://amzn.to/2rOVtqk

Notebook: Keep notes on my shipping weights, sizes and prices. This will help me get familiar with the actual costs, nationally and internationally. Compare prices on line between FedEx, UPS and USPS.

> 11" x 8.5"
> http://amzn.to/2ryTeaT
> 9.5" x 6"
> http://amzn.to/2s8eHEv
> 8" x 5"
> http://amzn.to/2qAJRHi
> 6" x 4"
> http://amzn.to/2sfzDc4

Also I'll take note of the time it takes me to 'Handle' my shipping.

Receipt File: Keep paper copies of my completed orders with shipping notes on them.

> 13.5" x 10"
> http://amzn.to/2qAzBdi
> 10.5" x 5.5"
> http://amzn.to/2s8mn9K

Shipping Sources:

> U.S. Postal Service:
> https://www.usps.com/
> United Parcel Service:
> https://www.ups.com/
> Federal Express:
> http://www.fedex.com/

The sooner you ship the order the better. It's important to put a realistic time frame on your listing as to when you can ship the order. Don't promise more than you can deliver, this upsets people like nothing else. In fact, customers are typically thrilled to get their order sooner than they expected and will often cite that as a plus in reviews.

You can schedule pickups of packages at your home by way of your shipper's website. If you don't have mail pick-up at your home or studio, find out from your local Post Office and shipping centers when their last daily drop-off time is to get a package out that day. This will help you to schedule your packing time. The more shipping you do, the better you'll get at it and you'll be able to easily quote someone the cost of shipping a particular item to anywhere in the world. Once you do ship your order, Etsy will send an automatic email with a tracking number to you and to your customer.

Track It To Understand It

Create a shipping spreadsheet or notebook for yourself so you can get familiar with how much it costs to ship your goods to different places. Measure and weigh your boxes and then spend some time online getting quotes, nationally and internationally. FedEx, UPS, and the US Postal Service all have websites where you can get a shipping quote without purchasing a label. If you are shipping through Etsy, they contract with the US Postal Service and FedEx, so you'll get a slightly better price than from those actual shipper websites. You can also sign up with Stamps.com, which offers discounted postage and label services. You'll need to research which shipping options work best for your particular business.

It's always more efficient in time and money if you are able to print your own labels. It's an easy process with Etsy and it beats standing in line at the Post Office. Once packed and labeled and if size allows, I recommend putting your boxes into reusable cloth shopping bags to transport your goods from the studio to the Post Office. Carrying your boxes in cloth bags make it so much easier when you have multiple orders going out.

Make friends with your local postal person! They can be very helpful with all of your shipping needs. Ask them for advice about any shipping information. Make sure you affix the label well, tape the box well, have a clear return address, and fragile stickers if appropriate.

I keep a paper copy of all Etsy Order Receipts so that I can easily refer to them if I need to. On those receipts I write notes about the order, like anything custom or if the buyer wanted me to send it as a gift, wrapped and with a personal note, etc. I also include the date I shipped it, the weight, and the cost. I have had to refer to a shipping receipt on a few occasions and it's been invaluable to have all of that information at my fingertips. Also, your shipping costs are tax-deductible and need to be tracked. Keeping receipts bodes well for you and your accountant.

Presentation Is Everything

When it comes to shipping, presentation is everything. This is often overlooked and can fare quite badly for your image. I once heard of an artist who sold an expensive piece of sculpture and then shipped it in a recycled diaper box. What?! While recycling is a good thing, this is unacceptable. Have some respect for your own work and how it arrives at someone's door! After the initial visual on the Internet, your shipped package is the second impression you will make on your customer, so make it a good one.

I do promote recycling and I use recycled

peanuts, bubble wrap and sometimes boxes if they are in good shape. Using social media, you can put a call out to your local friends and businesses for their used packing material. People are usually happy not to have to throw out that stuff, and it's a great way to save money on shipping supplies.

Since I make production pieces of only three sizes, I was able to figure out exactly the size of the boxes I needed. Having the right size boxes on hand whenever you need them is actually cost efficient too, as you won't be spending time looking for old boxes, cutting them down, or cleaning them up. This is a smart investment in your image too – have a nice box!

If you do use the same size boxes consistently, you can pre-enter the sizes of the boxes you use in Shipping Settings. This makes the label making process quick and easy. For The Quoted Cup, I designed my own return mailing label sticker with the company logo on it. This one was printed at Websticker.com and I was quite pleased with the quality and the customer service. Even though a printed shipping label includes my return address, my unique sticker is a visual reminder of my brand. It's the first thing the buyer will look at when they receive the box.

Also, in my case, Fragile stickers are a must. They are inexpensive and better than writing all over the box.

My typical box heading out to a customer.

A Gift For Your Customer To Open

What's inside the box is also aesthetically important. Use recycled packing material, but only when it's clean. Don't pack dusty or stained material around your beautiful craft. If your product is breakable, wrap it well and don't skimp on the packing material! It's not worth it if your piece breaks in transit. The general rule is to have at least two inches of packing material between the wrapped objects and the box. If it's really fragile, double boxing is an option with the same two-inch rule.

Include any necessary care instructions. Think about that – what you take for granted may not be obvious to the buyer. I now include a note about heating, cooling, and washing my cups. I started to do this after a customer dropped a star on her review because I had no care instructions. It hadn't occurred to me that not everyone knew how to take care of ceramics! That review was a learning experience worth its weight in gold!

Be sure to include a Thank You note to the buyer. Remember, they bought this piece from YOU, not a corporation, so a note is a nice personal touch. I also always include a business card. Some people even include a small seasonal gift, like a few pieces of candy at Halloween or Christmas. You might include something from the process of your work, like a stone or small clay tile. This is not necessary, but it is fun to surprise your customers if that's an easy thing for you to do.

The next photo is an example of what goes in the box by CakeArtbyChristy.com. They specialize in creating handcrafted royal icing decorations, helping DIY/novice bakers add an impressive accent to any home-baked delight. They include pretty colored tissue around their products and the owner created her own stamp for the cards that she hand writes for each order – it's a wonderful touch that accents their wonderful products.

Cake Art By Christy's handmade card, products and packing supplies.

You also want to ask your customer for a review. Reviews are essential to web-based businesses. Customers have up to 60 days from the purchase date to leave a review. The Etsy app will notify you if they did, if you set it up that way. Always read your reviews. This is how you learn how customers feel about your product and your business practices. I've improved many aspects of The Quoted Cup from customer suggestions. Don't miss the opportunity to ask your customer to help you out. Here's what's on the two-sided note that

I put in all of my boxes:

Thank you for your order!
The Quoted Cup uses recycled packaging whenever possible and encourages others to as well.

You can usually recycle unwanted shipping materials at your local shipping store.

If there is any damage when your order arrives, please save product and packaging and contact me immediately.

Taking Care of Your Quoted Cup.
Regular automatic dishwashing is fine but do not 'scrub' over the text while hand washing. The cup can be frozen to prepare for a cold beverage or microwaved for LESS than 2 minutes.

I hope you enjoy your handmade, one-of-a-kind, functional art!
I would love your feedback as it helps me grow my business!
Please take a few moments to leave me a review.
You'll find the link under "You > Your Purchases and Reviews."
Thanks so much! Mandy

Packing and shipping, or "handling", can take more time than you expect. Keep your shipping area stocked, clean, and organized and it will speed up your process. Every time you pack a box, it's proof that what you are doing is working! Yay!

*Be kind
whenever possible.
It is
always possible.*

DALAI LAMA

CUSTOMER SERVICE

In today's online world of commerce, customer service is king. It doesn't matter if you have the best of the best of the best product. If your customer is not happy, you are in trouble. Customer reviews are a tool we all shop with now. Whenever you buy an item that's new to you, don't you look for customer reviews? It's a pretty great way to feel more informed when you are handing your money over to a stranger.

As an entrepreneur, customer service is a chance for you to shine. You can go above and beyond what other sellers are doing to create a great relationship with your customer. It's often the littlest of things that make all the difference. For example, with The Quoted

Cup, I offer free gift-wrap and a handmade personal note if the buyer is sending their purchase as a gift. I use some simple colored tissue and handwrite their note on a nice, small piece of card stock. This takes only a few minutes more of my time yet goes a long way to make the buyer and the recipient feel happy and special. It also makes me feel good to do that for someone.

Communicate

It's important to pay attention to special requests that the customer makes when they order. Buyers are able to add comments in the "Note To Seller" section when they check out and their text will print on the order slip. I always reply right away with a confirmation that I received their custom request and ask any necessary clarifying questions. This quick response immediately puts customers at ease and starts our business relationship off in the right direction.

Your customer is who pays your bills and you want them to be happy. If they are, you want them to tell everyone by leaving you that review. As well as putting a review request note in the box, you can send them an email or conversation in Etsy (aka convo). Wait at least a week and don't be too pushy.

A happy customer is a potential return customer, and a return customer is your best customer. That being said, the customer is *not* always right and you'll have to make choices on how to proceed when things don't go well… and yes, there will be times when things don't go well. From a wrong address, to breakage or theft, to just an unhappy human at the other end of the line, your "people skills" will be called into action.

It's Your Problem First

Mistakes happen, on both sides. When something goes wrong or a customer is not happy, always respond quickly and professionally. Never bring emotion into the situation. Even if the problem is not your fault, it's ultimately easier and more effective to just focus on remedying the issue.

Do you want to be right or do you want to be happy?

What you want is to move on with your business and your life. So choose your battles wisely and always stay professional. Sometimes it's easiest to just replace the item or refund the purchase and move on. In my case, every once in awhile, something breaks in shipping or the wrong cup got in the box. I ask for a photo of the cup and then I don't hesitate to immediately send a replacement. Done and done. Even if it's not your fault, you have to ask yourself how much your own time is it worth and go on from there.

At the time of this writing, I have garnered almost 1,800 Etsy sales and over 420 customer reviews, and all but three are 5-star. I'm pretty proud of that and I've worked hard for it. Of those three, less than 5-star reviews, all of them ended up being rather funny stories, and the situations were out of my control.

One was a woman who blasted me negatively in a posted review as soon as she received her cup, without contacting me first. Her exact words were, "When I opened the box I was horrified..." Um, really, horrified? Ok that's some strong language about a cup, especially considering the state of the world today. I got back to her immediately and worked diligently with her, through many Etsy conversations or "convos", to understand the situation. After numerous confusing exchanges as to why she was so displeased, the last one stated "...and my son doesn't even drink beer, only milk, so this mug is useless!" Aaah, ok, I get it now... maybe she's "not all there" and there is just no pleasing her. At this point I actually contacted Etsy management and after reviewing all of our convos, they removed her review.

Another time the Post Office as well as the customer were to blame. A shipment meant for western Canada was inexplicably rerouted from Los Angeles to Brazil then Florida then New York, and eventually, almost three months later, came back to me in New Mexico. I re-shipped it immediately. All the while I was in constant contact with the customer, tracking the package and giving him updates. I attempted to point out the funny irony of his "cup on a road trip" which was only mildly successful. He was irritated to say the least and made sure to convey that to me. But I never responded negatively. As it turned out, he had made a small mistake on the address, which started the whole problem. But I knew better than to dwell on that fact. I just sent his order to the corrected address as soon as I could. So, mistakes do happen and you just do your best to remedy them as quickly as possible.

Embrace Your Power

Customer service is actually a favorite part of my business. I love the chance I get to make people who I've never met happy and to add a little functional beauty to their lives as well. I love that customers go out of their way to write nice things about my work and their buying experience with me in their reviews. Leaving a review is something I now take time for when I buy products, because I know how important that is to the seller. I love that my work is in homes in Canada, England, Ireland, Poland, Australia, Norway, Sweden, and across the United States. I am always grateful for every customer.

It does not matter
how slowly you go,
as long as
you do not stop.

CONFUCIUS

BE PATIENT AND GROW

I started my Etsy shop in 2009, but it wasn't then anything like it is now. The evolution of The Quoted Cup has happened over many years. I've learned so much about running a business through the Etsy platform; it's been like a paid education. Because it is so inexpensive to run, I was able to take my time and learn as I went. I got better at making my work and perfecting my product and my brand. I got better at customer service, shipping, and sourcing materials. And I did all of that while working other jobs. The Quoted Cup was sometimes part-time and sometimes full-time, depending on seasons and sales. And all of this experience informs my fine art world as well.

I suggest you use Etsy as a learning tool, as an inexpensive education. This is not just a selling platform, but a community of like-minded artisans as well. There are tens of thousands of people just like you who are also figuring it out. Take time to read articles in the *Seller Handbook*. Follow the posts and ask questions if you need to in the Forums. Spend time perusing other shops to get ideas. There is a wealth of information on Etsy's site for you to use. Etsy wants you to be successful, because that's what makes them successful.

Evolve At Your Own Pace

Set attainable goals. Once your shop is up and running, create small, achievable objectives. Focus on getting your first sale within three months. Make time to work your shop. You can't just set it and forget it if you want it to thrive. Just like a job working for someone else, you need to show up, which means you need to schedule the time that you are working for you. If you check in consistently throughout the week, you'll get better at running your shop. Just like a relationship or a garden, your business needs to be nurtured in order to thrive.

Not only do you need to make the product, you need to learn to get it out there and sell it.

Marketing can be tricky, but it's nothing you can't be taught by doing. Be willing to evolve. Taos Gargirl turned into the successful Quoted Cup because that's the direction it organically went. I couldn't have conceived then of what it is now when it first started. That doesn't mean I didn't have a vision of what I wanted it to be, it just means that I allowed my vision to be malleable so that it could grow.

You Are Ready

Congratulations, you are ready to be an entrepreneur! If you've gone through this book and set yourself up, you should be proud! Often, just getting started is the hardest part. Now you are qualified to keep growing as an entrepreneur. Educate yourself outside of Etsy as well. There are literally endless sources of information on the web on how to run a successful business.

But more than seeking business advice, also research how to "stay in the game" when it comes to your own thoughts. Sticking it out when the going gets tough can be hard. Don't get discouraged, get educated! Most creative people struggle with some level of fear and uncertainty when it comes to their work. This is normal. We must learn to separate ourselves from the work we make. It's a big world out there and we are all an important part of it. Being in control of our thoughts is the most powerful tool we have to succeed in any area of our life.

The World is Your Oyster

The great thing about "self help" sources is the obvious opportunity to learn how to *help yourself*. I recommend the business, money, and personal growth knowledge from any of the following people to get started with: Anthony Robbins, Marie Forleo, Richard Branson, Kyle Cease, Danielle LaPorte, Ash Ambirge, Barbara Stanny and Kate Northrup just to name a few. There are, of course, many more, and your search will lead you where you need to go.

Remember your Whys. What is your mission statement? This should be posted somewhere in your workspace where you can see it everyday. You are an artist. You have vision. You have something to give back to the world. Your job, no matter what, is to honor your gifts and share them. So go forth and conquer! Do your work, make your money, and change the world!

RESOURCES

The resources listed below ~ and more ~ can be found at www.FromArtisticToEntrepreneur.com

40 Free Listings on Etsy:
www.FromArtisticToEntrepreneur.com

The Quoted Cup store on Etsy:
www.etsy.com/shop/TheQuotedCup

My fine art website: www.mandystapleford.com

Learn how to publish your own book here:
http://bit.ly/2pdNP85

Etsy: www.Etsy.com

Worksheets

Worksheet #1: MY WHYS
Worksheet #2: MY TIME
Worksheet #3: MY OUTCOMES
Worksheet #4: MY MONEY
Worksheet #5: MY SHOP
Worksheet #6: MY SHIPPING

Note: all worksheets can be downloaded at
www.FromArtisticToEntrepreneur.com

Videos & Interviews

Kyle Cease on Meditation: http://bit.ly/2psvtfW

Simon Sinek on Why: http://bit.ly/2qTo21p

Marie Forleo Interviews Elizabeth Gilbert on
Big Magic: http://bit.ly/2pZxUYd

Tony Robbins on Productivity and
Paperwork: http://bit.ly/2qTFfrH

Elizabeth Gilbert on Creative Genius:
http://bit.ly/2pUnhrJ

Books

Money, a Love Story by Kate Northrup

Purple Cow by Seth Godin

Big Magic by Elizabeth Gilbert

The Big Leap by Gay Hendricks

Printing

Printing for Business Cards: www.vistaprint.com

Custom Labels: www.websticker.com

Equipment & Supplies

A complete list of shipping supplies, cards, and the lighting equipment I use can be found on the website at:
www.FromArtisticToEntrepreneur.com

ABOUT THE AUTHOR

Mandy Lee works as an artist and writer and is a serial entrepreneur. Never idle, she juggles multiple business projects... combining her creativity and commerce as a path to self-employment and personal freedom. She wrote this book to inspire others to overcome their obstacles and take more control of their own lives through entrepreneurship. She lives in Taos, New Mexico with her husband, three dogs, and three fish.

Made in the USA
Coppell, TX
25 May 2020

26429538R20085